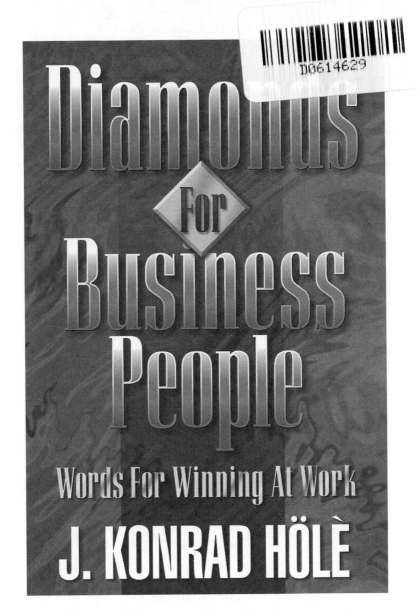

Diamonds For Business People

Words For Winning At Work

J. KONRAD HÖLÈ

Proverbs 4:7 says, "Wisdom is the Principle thing." Wisdom is the only proof that you are being **"Mentored"** by the **"Most Intelligent Person In The Universe,"** the "Holy Spirit."

Unless otherwise indicated, all Scripture quotations are taken from the King James Version of the Bible.

Diamonds for Business People

Copyright © 1996 by J. Konrad Hölè
ISBN 1-888696-01-X
World Centre Ministries
P.O. Box 41010
Minneapolis, MN 55441

Published by
The World Press
P.O. Box 41010
Minneapolis, MN 55441

Foreword

I realized that the closer I became to the **"Holy Spirit,"** who is the **"Spirit of Wisdom,"** not only would He teach me everything He knows, but He would ignite a craving within me to know more. You will never remember someone's **"Words,"** as much as you will remember someone's **"Point."** That is why I wrote this book. It is simply because I believe that one **"Diamond Key"** of wisdom can unlock a **"Vaulted Treasure"** of information.

You and I are only ever **"One Truth"** away from what we do not understand, and what we need to know. These are not copies of someone else's quotes, or revelation. These are **"Diamonds of Revelation"** that the "Holy Spirit" has unlocked to me in Crusades, Seminars, and Teachings around the world. Feel free to share these with someone that needs to know what you know.

Diamonds are not just a **"Girl's Bestfriend,"** they're everybody's **"BESTFRIEND."**

Enjoy.

J. Konrad

Dedication

This collection of **"Diamonds"** is dedicated first and foremost to: My **"Incredible Wife"** Kristina, whose merciful, graceful, and peace-making nature graciously balances out the perfectionist driven, absolutely decisive, and always opinionated volcano that she married! If I had it to do over again, I'd still pick you. You're wonderful.

My **"Dearest Friend and Mentor,"** Dr. Mike Murdock who would always tell me, "If you can't get to the point, don't go on the journey." Thank you, MM, for teaching me how to get to the **"Point"** so quickly.

And most of all, my most **"Precious Companion,"** the **"Holy Spirit,"** who patiently and gently does not stop polishing **"My Coals,"** until they become **"His Diamonds."** You're the Greatest!

Table of Contents

Appearance

1. People will see you, before they hear you.

2. Look good to yourself. You can't win if you feel like a loser.

3. Get a photograph of where you want to be physically, financially, fashionably, and intellectually, and build every day around it.

4. Your **Appearance** is the platform for your presentation.

5. Study "Class." Sloppiness is not an excuse for individuality.

6. Never give others the "true **Appearance**" of "false information."

7. **Appear** reachable. No one will reach for you, if they don't believe they can touch you.

Diamond Words

*A merry heart maketh a cheerful countenance:
but by sorrow of the heart the spirit is broken
Proverbs 15:13*

Associations

1 The seed you sow in others will determine the harvest you reap from them.

2 Never link yourself to those walking outside their assignment.

3 Those walking in disobedience, attract those comfortable with disobedience.

4 Ethical people link with other ethical people because iron sharpens iron. Unethical people link with other unethical people because there is no threat by truth to expose error.

5 Never allow uninvited restless people to wander into your life.

6 Those that do not build anything in your life, will eventually tear something down.

7 Every person you become connected to, has other **Associations** in their life just like them.

Diamond Words

Blessed is the man that walketh not in the counsel of the ungodly, nor standeth in the way of sinners... Psalms 1:1

Attitude

1 Your **Attitude** will determine your altitude.

2 Excellence is the endeavor to be efficient, not the excuse to be arrogant.

3 When you respond to ignorance, you perpetuate it.

4 Never mistake success as the opportunity to be a snob.

5 Your **Attitude** must say who you are, not who you are not.

6 Treat everyone with respect. You never know when the "errand boy" will become the "President"!

7 What you display to others, will be what they believe about you.

Diamond Words

Let the words of my mouth, and the meditation of my heart, be acceptable in thy sight, O LORD, my strength, and my redeemer   Psalms 19:14

Communication

1 Your words will either build a platform to stand on, or dig a ditch to fall in.

2 Speak from your passion, not from someone else's.

3 Words are the only opportunity you have to enter someone's moment, and change their lifetime.

4 Say in a sentence, what others say in a paragraph.

5 If you cannot arrive at the point, don't go on the journey.

6 Allow your mind to load the gun, before you allow your mouth to pull the trigger.

7 **Communication** is the ability to take people on a journey from where they are, to where they need to be.

Diamond Words

*Let no corrupt **Communication** proceed out of your mouth; but that which is good to the use of edifying   Ephesians 4:29*

Creativity

1 Great leaders use their mind for **Creativity**, not memory.

2 Great leaders look to desire "Conception," and focus for "Completion."

3 Be married to a result, not a method.

4 **Creativity** Births. Structure Completes.

5 Your "Biggest Successes" are just a collection of "Small Adjustments."

6 **Creativity** is an individuality, that similarity will never be.

7 You will only maintain productivity, as long as you protect **Creativity**.

Diamond Words

...My heart is inditing a good matter: I speak of the things which I have made touching the king: my tongue is the pen of a ready writer. Psalms 45:1

Criticism

1 **Criticism** is just anothers way of envying your progress, and despising your difference.

2 Often times when others **Criticize** you it's because they see in you the boldness to be a "stone," instead of the fear in themselves to just be a piece of the rock.

3 Never defend your creativity to someone who is **Critical**.

4 **Criticism** is a reaction of those who are intimidated in being "out done," more than motivated towards getting "more done."

5 Champions strategize, losers **Criticize**.

6 Those not making suggestions for your improvement, are unqualified to **Criticize** your achievements.

7 **Criticism** will never destroy you, if it's not allowed to control you.

— D i a m o n d   W o r d s —

Having a good conscience; that, whereas they speak evil of you, as of evildoers, they may be ashamed that falsely accuse... I Peter 3:16

Debt

1 **Debt** will put you in intentional situations, that blessings will have to bail you out of.

2 **Debt** says you believe *God* to pay back more than to provide.

3 **Debt** takes the right to exercise covenant promise out of *God's* hands.

4 **Debt** makes you a prisoner to pressure, and a stranger to faith.

5 **Debt** is not a sign of growth, it's a sign of doubt.

6 Everything *God* has called you to do, *He* will pay for you to do it.

7 Hate **Debt** as much as sin.

Diamond Words

For the LORD thy God blesseth thee, as he promised thee: and thou shalt lend unto many nations, but thou shalt not borrow...
Deuteronomy 15:6

Decisions

1 Your **Decisions** determine your circumstances. If you don't like your circumstances, change your **Decisions**.

2 You will only make wrong **Decisions** from wrong information.

3 "Pig Pens" are the result of a **Decision** to go somewhere *God* did not tell you to.

4 You will never be more celebrated with "Right **Decisions**" and never more isolated with "Wrong Ones."

5 Every **Decision** will either showcase your achievements, or your regrets.

6 Today's **Decisions** determine tomorrow's provisions.

7 Never be so loyal to a wrong **Decision**, that you refuse to let repentance reverse it.

───── D i a m o n d   W o r d s ─────

And thine ears shall hear a word behind thee, saying, This is the way, walk ye in it...
Isaiah 30:21

Diligence

Diligence to instruction increases responsibility.

Diligence to detail increases dependability.

Diligence to wisdom increases durability.

Diligence to problem-solving increases reward-ability.

Diligence to assignment increases achievability.

Diligence to organization increases productivity.

Diligence to focus removes instability.

Diamond Words

*Seest thou a man **Diligent** in his business? he shall stand before kings; he shall not stand before mean men   Proverbs 22:29*

Excellence

1 **Excellence** will cost you what mediocrity will save you.

2 **Excellent** people will conquer, what average people will complain about.

3 **Excellent** people pursue solutions, average people stare at problems.

4 **Excellence** orchestrates in your mind, translates in your speech, and demonstrates in your life.

5 Others will notice your effort to be **Excellent**, more than your acceptance to be mediocre.

6 Never expect someone else to tolerate the same lack of **Excellence,** that you would not.

7 Make improvements, not excuses.

Diamond Words

In all things showing thyself a pattern of good works: in doctrine showing uncorruptness, gravity, sincerity   Titus 2:7

Failure

1 **Failure** is not final. It's a temporary delay, not a permanent defeat.

2 **Failures** just expose what doesn't work, so you can focus your pursuit on what will.

3 The pain of **Failure** will stay with you, until the photograph of starting over supersedes it.

4 *God* uses the devastation of your setbacks, as the preparation for your comebacks.

5 Champions learn from defeat, losers live in it.

6 **Failure** is never possible, unless it's considered.

7 When man sees your **Failures**, he sees your end. When *God* sees your **Failures**, *He* sees your beginning.

— D i a m o n d   W o r d s —

Though he fall, he shall not be utterly cast down: for the LORD upholdeth him with his hand
Psalms 37:24

Favor

1. **Favor** is the ability to get what you need, without having to do what you thought to get it.

2. If you don't sow **Favor**, you won't reap it.

3. The difference between where you are, and where you would like to be, is determined by somebody who can get you there.

4. You cannot buy with money, what **Favor** can give to you.

5. One person that celebrates you is worth more than a thousand people that tolerate you.

6. Somebody is walking around with a blessing, and they are trying to find YOU!

7. You are only one "Boaz" away from the barley fields to the palace.

Diamond Words

For thou, LORD, wilt bless the righteous; with Favour wilt thou compass him as with a shield   Psalms 5:12

Focus

1 You will never have a platform for your achievements, until you have a fortress around your **Focus**.

2 If you can change your **Focus**, you can change your failure.

3 Your **Focus** will offend those not permitted to distract it.

4 If your enemy can have your **Focus**, he can have your life.

5 No one else will guard your **Focus**, you will have to.

6 If your enemy can keep your **Focus** on the land of problem, he can keep you out of the land of promise.

7 Those who do not value your **Focus**, will not value your assignment either.

Diamond Words

Looking unto Jesus the author and finisher of our faith; who for the joy that was set before him endured... Hebrews 12:2

Goals

1 Be realistic. You can't achieve what you can't believe.

2 Be married to the **Goal**, not the plan.

3 Learn to eat a cow, a steak at a time.

4 Build your team with completers, as well as thinkers.

5 Always know where you are in proximity to achievement.

6 If you don't have a **Goal**, you will never have a future.

7 If you don't reach for something, you will settle for anything, and achieve nothing.

Diamond Words

For which of you, intending to build a tower, sitteth not down first, and counteth the cost, whether he have sufficient to finish it?
Luke 14:28

Habits

1 Success and failure are separated by the kind of **Habits** you follow daily.

2 Champions realize that their preparation determines their destination.

3 **Habits** are forceful. The bad ones can hurt you, as much as the good ones can help you.

4 You can only qualify a **Habit** by looking at the future it will produce.

5 You cannot stop a wrong **Habit,** until you start a right one.

6 It only requires a few "right things" in your day to make a lot of "right things" happen in your life.

7 **Habits** are made to order. You must decide the ones that work best for you.

Diamond Words

So will I sing praise unto thy name for ever, that I may daily perform my vows   Psalms 61:8

Information

❖ **Information** narrows the gap between where you are, and where you want to be.

❖ Always obtain enough **Information** to make a qualified decision.

❸ The kind of **Information** you lack, is contained in the kind of questions you ask.

❹ Never try to use partial **Information** to make a whole point.

❺ Make **Information** accessible. What you can't find, you can't use.

❖ The wise identify what they lack, and go after those who possess it.

❖ You are always one piece of **Information** away from a breakthrough.

D i a m o n d   W o r d s

The entrance of thy words giveth light; it giveth understanding unto the simple
Psalms 119:130

Loyalty

1 **Loyalty** is a gift you cannot buy from another, or sell yourself.

2 **Loyalty** is not what you promise, it's what you practice.

3 Reward **Loyalty**. If it doesn't become important, it may become absent.

4 Those that do not guard others, will not guard you.

5 Stand behind your word, not away from it.

6 A person's motives will answer the questions for their existence.

7 The moment you can purchase **Loyalty**, is the moment it can be sold for a higher price.

——— D i a m o n d W o r d s ———

Faithful are the wounds of a friend; but the kisses of an enemy are deceitful   Proverbs 27:6

Motivation

1 Improvements are only as quick, as your **Motivation** to correct deficiency.

2 Inferiority that is **Motivated**, will go further than superiority that is complacent.

3 Complacency never starts "big." It begins "small" and gains momentum.

4 The brick wall is not a sign your enemy has stopped you, it is a sign you have not found the door yet.

5 **Motivation** is what destroys complacency, and determines tenacity.

6 You will never be **Motivated** by anothers vision, unless it's your vision.

7 Move towards those who "energize where you are going," more than "sympathize with where you have come from."

─── Diamond Words ───

Be strong and of a good courage...for the LORD thy God, he it is that doth go with thee; he will not fail thee, nor forsake thee   Deuteronomy 31:6

Observation

① **Observation** will reveal what education cannot.

② **Observe** how great people handle great adversity.

③ Whatever you can **Observe**, you can understand. Whatever you can understand you can master.

④ If you can **Observe** your environment, you can position yourself to handle it.

⑤ Discernment is the *Holy Spirit's* way to allow you to see things as they really are, instead of how they appear to be.

⑥ You can't stop the flood, until you can **Observe** the leak.

⑦ Watch when others don't think you're watching. Listen when others don't think you're listening.

――――――― D i a m o n d   W o r d s ―――――――
*For Herod feared John, knowing that he was a just man and an holy, and **Observed** him; and when he heard him, he did many things, and heard him gladly   Mark 6:20*

Organization

1 The longer you live with disorder, the longer you will live with the pain it produces.

2 When something is in the right place, it can produce the right results.

3 **Organization** will never begin, until the pain of clutter becomes too overwhelming.

4 **Organize** your structure around what works best for who you are, and where you are at.

5 If people don't know their position, they will never know their purpose.

6 **Organize** your goals with an ending, not just a beginning.

7 The first step towards **Organization**, is the honesty to admit something is out of place.

D i a m o n d   W o r d s

For God is not the author of confusion, but of peace, as in all churches of the saints
I Corinthians 14:33

People

People are *God's* way of "blessing" you, and the enemy's way of "stressing" you.

People are *God's* way of helping you over, and the enemy's way of keeping you under.

People are *God's* way of adding to your assignment, and the enemy's way of distracting it.

People are *God's* way of supporting your strengths, and the enemy's way of distorting your weaknesses.

People are *God's* link to your future, and your enemy's link to your past.

If a person's words cannot survive interrogation, they are unqualified for consideration.

Never reach for those not reaching.

——— D i a m o n d   W o r d s ———

*He that walketh with wise men shall be wise:
but a companion of fools shall be destroyed
Proverbs 13:20*

Preparation

1 If you don't **Prepare** to succeed, you will prepare to fail.

2 The absence of **Preparation** will bring the presence of devastation.

3 *God* can change your direction, but you must **Prepare** to go somewhere first.

4 You will never reach completion unless you have **Prepared** a map to the finish line.

5 Write your plans. You cannot run with a thought.

6 **Preparation** says that you are planning to succeed in what you are doing.

7 **Prepare** with what you have. Have faith for what you don't, and you will achieve what you could not.

D i a m o n d   W o r d s
---

*The **Preparations** of the heart in man, and the answer of the tongue, is from the LORD*
Proverbs 16:1

Pressure

1 **Pressure** is the proof you are spending your life trying to live up to another's standards.

2 *God's* instructions will produce faith, your ideas will produce **Pressure**.

3 Wise counsel relieves the **Pressure** of wrong decisions.

4 **Pressure** is magnified when facilitating a wrong idea.

5 Stress is the proof you are not doing things *God's* way.

6 **Pressure** will only be as big as what you decide to tolerate.

7 If you walk in character, you will never be under **Pressure** of trying to hide your actions.

—— D i a m o n d   W o r d s ——

It is vain for you to rise up early, to sit up late, to eat the bread of sorrows: for so he giveth his beloved sleep   Psalms 127:2

Problem-Solving

1 Never complain about anything you won't attempt to solve.

2 Average people point out problems, excellent people solve them.

3 Those that never get involved, never get promoted.

4 Those who do not solve problems, start them.

5 **Problem-Solving** is determined by the willingness to react, more than the carelessness to observe.

6 Problems you are incapable of solving, will not stand out to you.

7 Diplomacy is the harbor through the storms of commitment.

Diamond Words

Without counsel purposes are disappointed: but in the multitude of counsellors they are established   Proverbs 15:22

Pursuit

1 Never ask *God* to give you something, you are unwilling to go after.

2 You will never possess something until the **Pursuit** of going after it, overwhelms the passivity of living without it.

3 Present **Pursuit**, will require you to move through memories of past failures.

4 **Pursuit** will require you to take a step with nothing.

5 **Pursuit** begins with your desire, not anothers permission.

6 **Pursuit** silences regret from creating photographs of what you could have had, had you **Pursued**.

7 When you want something you have never had, you have got to do something you have never done. (Dr. Mike Murdock)

--- Diamond Words ---

For every one that asketh receiveth; and he that seeketh findeth; and to him that knocketh it shall be opened   Matthew 7:8

Questions

1 **Questions** reveal the humility to acknowledge something you don't know, and the hunger to find it.

2 Those who never ask, never learn.

3 You must identify the information you need, before you can qualify the **Questions** to get it.

4 Those who never interrogate greatness, never become great.

5 Specific information can only be accessed by specific **Questions**.

6 Intimate information, can only be accessed by considerate **Questions.**

7 Those that hate interrogation, hate information.

————— D i a m o n d W o r d s —————

If any of you lack wisdom, let him ask of God, that giveth to all men liberally, and upbraideth not; and it shall be given him.
James 1:5

Relationship

1 When *God* wants to birth a future, *He* births a **Relationship**. When the enemy wants to destroy a future, he births a **Relationship**.

2 Unnecessary **Relationships** produce unrealistic expectations.

3 Opposition is never present until multiplication is possible.

4 You will be known as much for the people you avoid, as much as the ones you associate with.

5 Never attempt to take people past the "expiration date" of their seasons in your life.

6 Celebrate the "Seasons" *God* puts people in your life, and the "Reasons" *He* takes them out.

7 Don't be a "pack rat" of wrong people.

D i a m o n d   W o r d s

Be ye not unequally yoked together with unbelievers: for what fellowship hath righteousness with unrighteousness?... II Corinthians 6:14

Resources

1 You will never reach for the expertise of others, until you acknowledge your own weakness.

2 The sacrifice of something you want, will determine the possession of something you want more.

3 Never ask directions, from someone who does not understand where you are going.

4 The life long "School of Wisdom" has varied teachers. Dip your pail in the wells of many.

5 Those you become linked to, are those you will imitate.

6 The moment you invite corrupt individuals into your assignment, is the moment you invite their tragedy to sabotage it.

7 If you could succeed alone, you would have already reached the top!

D i a m o n d   W o r d s

Go to the ant, thou sluggard; consider her ways, and be wise: Which having no guide, overseer, or ruler, Provideth her meat in the summer, and gathereth her food in the harvest. Proverbs 6:6-8

Schedule

1 If you don't plan your **Schedule**, you will be dominated by someone else's.

2 Those that will distract your **Schedule**, are those that do not have one themselves.

3 **Schedule** something daily that you love to do, as much as you **Schedule** something daily that you have to do.

4 If you do not value time, you will never value your assignment.

5 Unless you value your own **Schedule**, you will never be considerate of someone else's.

6 **Schedule** the exit of something, at the same time you **Schedule** the entrance.

7 When you document your day, you determine the strategies for tomorrow.

—— D i a m o n d   W o r d s ——

Redeeming the time, because the days are evil
Ephesians 5:16

Strength

1 **Strength** is determined by focus. What you look at either motivates you, or stagnates you.

2 Never use the **Strength** for achieving your goal, convincing others to believe in it.

3 Disconnect from those who "sympathize" where you are at, and move towards those who "energize" where you are going.

4 You will use more **Strength** pursuing an option, than you will following an instruction.

5 What you have a "love for," you will have a "longevity in."

6 **Strength** must be "daily renewed," or it will be "eventually expired."

7 The strategy to replace a mistake, comes from the honesty to admit you made one.

——— D i a m o n d   W o r d s ———

*But they that wait upon the LORD shall renew their **Strength**; they shall mount up with wings as eagles; they shall run, and not be weary; and they shall walk, and not faint   Isaiah 40:31*

Success

1 **Success** is not immunity from adversity, it's just the proof you conquered it.

2 **Success** is a reward for staying focused.

3 **Successful** people are just former failures who changed their focus.

4 Savor your **Successes**. You will always have time to ponder your mistakes.

5 You will only keep your **Successes** as long as you keep your focus.

6 **Success** is not measured in the size of your assignment, it's measured in the "obedience to your assignment."

7 The difference between **Success** and failure is what you master.

--- Diamond Words ---

This book of the law shall not depart out of thy mouth; but thou shalt meditate therein day and night,...and then thou shalt have good success Joshua 1:8

Signs & Wonders Partners

· ·

I want ot take this time and personally say how *"Excited"* and *"Grateful"* I am to God for the many friends from all parts of these United States that have become linked to this *Ministry of the Holy Spirit* with their prayers and with their monthly seed into this fertile soil of this harvest field. Having the privilege of the taking the message of this *"Wonderful Companion"* to thousands around the country in both live crusades and media outreach, has been a joy that words cannot express.

I know there are still yet many of you that *God's voice* is going to speak to, to become connected with this ministry as a special *"Signs and Wonders Partner"* both prayerfully and financially to help take this message of knowing the *Holy Spirit* to so many that still need to hear it.

Would you ask the *Holy Spirit* today about becoming linked with me at *$10.00 each month*, or whatever *He* lays upon your heart so we can reach this critical objective together. Remember, *whenever you react to His voice, He reacts to your future*.

I'll look forward to hearing from you.

☐ **Yes, J. Konrad I want to link myself to you with my monthly seed of $_____ a month for the spreading of this needed message around the world!**

Name _____

Address _____

City _____ State _____ Zip _____

Phone (_____)_____

Clip & Mail To: Spirit & Life Ministries
P.O. BOX 41010   MINNEAPOLIS, MN 55441

Let Me Agree With You In Prayer For Your Need!

You are daily upon my heart and your needs matter greatly to me. Don't ever think that you are alone. I want to agree with you that the Holy Spirit will bring the provision of God in your life!

Name _____

Address _____

City _____ State _____ Zip _____

Phone ( ) _____

Clip & Mail To: Spirit & Life Ministries
P.O. BOX 41010 MINNEAPOLIS, MN 55441

Clip & Mail

More Power-Packed Teaching From J. Konrad Hölè

The Leading Of His Spirit

Join J. Konrad for this "Explosive" and "In-Depth" study on how the Holy Spirit leads you more by "Purpose, Principals and Protocal" than He does by Euphoria, Emotion, and Excitement. The greatest seasons of your life are just ahead, LED BY HIS SPIRIT.
$20.00 (4 tape series)

In His Presence

Find out the life changing secrets of Kind David's revelation of how to live in the Presence of God. The most incredible breakthroughs in your life are about to take place just be being in His Presence.
$15.00 (3 tape series)

Diary Of The Holy Spirit

Discover the benefits of how to Commune, Flow, Discern, and Listen to the Holy Spirit who Jesus said would be with you Always. Your greatest relationship is one revelation away.
$15.00 (3 tape series)

Misery

Discover David's revelation principles from Psalms 16:11, that the only true place of joy was in God's presence, and that anything outside His presence was not designed to satisfy you, but rather would be a source of "Misery."
$20.00 (4 tape series)

The Mentor And The Protege

What is a *Mentor*? A gift by *God* to insure the success of completing your *Assignment*. What is a *Protege*? A person whose future depends on the impartation from somebody who has already been where they are going. In this impactive teaching you will understand the purpose of mentoring.
$20.00 (4 tape series)

"The Diamond Library for Achievers"
Several Dynamic Topics:

Build Your Complete Achiever Library!

Obedience

Join J. Konrad for this "Impactive" study on the "Power" of OBEDIENCE and its ability to be the bridge from "Where You Are," to "Where You Want To Be ," and God's ability to react to your life everytime you follow one of "His Instructions."
$10.00 (2 tapes)

Time

Join J. Konrad for this "Impactive" study on the "Currency of TIME," its ability to form your "Destiny" around you, and its critical role in developing your relationship with the Holy Spirit.
$10.00 (2 tapes)

Focus

Join J. Konrad for this "Impactive" study on the Force of "FOCUS," and its ability to enable you to walk through the "Valleys of Distraction," and complete your life assignment!
$10.00 (2 tapes)

Send Your Order In Today!

Seed-Faith

Join J. Konrad for this "Impactive" study on the "Power Of Seed Movement" in your life, and your ability to take something God has placed in your hand, to create something God has ordained in your life.
$10.00 (2 tapes)

Warfare

Join J. Konrad for this "Impactive" study of how you were not called to be a "Captive," you were called to be a "Deliverer."
$10.00 (2 tapes)

Direction

Join J. Konrad for this "Impactive" study on how the "HOLY SPIRIT" answers one of the most pivotal questions ever in your life... the question of DIRECTION.!
$10.00 (2 tapes)

SPECIAL PACKAGE PRICE... Receive all 6 titles into your life for just $30. (please specify when ordering)

Don't let these opportunities pass you by! Rush your order in today. Fill out the form below. Please print clearly and legibly. Ask the Holy Spirit what Seed He would have you to sow into this world-changing ministry.

Title	Qty.	Price	Total
The Leading Of His Spirit (Tapes)		$	$
In His Presence (Tapes)		$	$
The Diary Of The Holy Spirit (Tapes)		$	$
Misery (Tapes)		$	$
The Mentor And The Protege (Tapes)		$	$
Library For Achievers - Time (Tapes)		$	$
Library For Achievers - Obedience (Tapes)		$	$
Library For Achievers - Focus (Tapes)		$	$
Library For Achievers - Seed-Faith (Tapes)		$	$
Library For Achievers - Warfare (Tapes)		$	$
Library For Achievers - Direction (Tapes)		$	$

1 Item .... $2 - S/H   Shipping/Handling $
2 Items .... $3 - S/H   Seed-Faith Gift $
3 or more Items ..... $4 - S/H   Total $

☐ J. Konrad, please send me my **FREE** copy of your *Spirit & Life Talk* newsletter.

☐ Check ☐ Money Order ☐ Visa ☐ MasterCard

Card No. ☐☐☐☐☐☐☐☐☐☐☐☐☐☐☐☐

Exp. Date _____ Signature _____

Name _____

Address _____

City _____ State _____ Zip _____

Phone (____) _____

Clip & Mail To: Spirit & Life Ministries
P.O. BOX 41010 MINNEAPOLIS, MN 55441

Clip & Mail

Choose From These Exciting Titles! Books that will bring a Breakthrough... Your life will be challenged and changed with revelation knowledge!

Diamonds For Daily Living

Diamonds For Ministers

Diamonds For Mothers

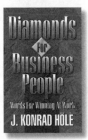

Diamonds For Business People

You Were Born A Champion... Don't Die A Loser!

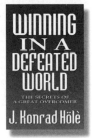

Winning In A Defeated World

Leading In the Midst Of Followers

Living Large In A Small World

See the next page for details on how to order your personal copies of these books!

"Literature Evangelism Team"

Order Form

☐ Yes, J. Konrad, I want to be a part of this "Evangelism Breakthrough" so that I may affect those that God links me to with the power of revelation knowledge.

Order a set of 10 copies of any title for $10. You may also mix titles of the books to bring a total of 10 copies for $10. Order for your friends and family!

Title	Qty. (Sets of 10)	Price	Total
Diamonds For Daily Living		x $10	$
Diamonds For Ministers		x $10	$
Diamonds For Mothers		x $10	$
Diamonds For Business People		x $10	$
You Were Born A Champion...		x $10	$
Winning In A Defeated World		x $10	$
Leading In The Midst Of Followers		x $10	$
Living Large In A Small World		x $10	$
		Shipping	$
Add $2 For Shipping		Seed-Faith Gift	$
		Total	$

☐ Check   ☐ Money Order   ☐ Visa   ☐ MasterCard

Card No. ☐☐☐☐☐☐☐☐☐☐☐☐☐☐☐☐☐☐☐☐

Exp. Date _____ Signature _____

Name _____

Address _____

City _____ State _____ Zip _____

Phone (   ) _____

Clip & Mail To: Spirit & Life Ministries
P.O. BOX 41010   MINNEAPOLIS, MN 55441

Clip & Mail